For beachcombers
young and old.

Copyright ©2015 by Molly Montgomery. All rights reserved. No part of this book may be used or reproduced in any manner whatsoever without written permission from the author, except in the case of brief quotations embodied in critical articles and reviews.

Book design, photographs and illustrations by Molly Montgomery

Printed in the United States of America
First print edition: July 2015
ISBN-13: 978-1508473107
ISBN-10: 1508473102

There are so many cool things
to see on the beaches of Kachemak Bay.
Let's take a walk and see
what we find . . .

Eagle feather

Eagle feather

Ee

Whelks

Whelks

ww

Alaska Fish and Game Tide Pool Etiquette:

1. **Walk, don't run.** You may trip and fall in unfamiliar terrain. Walking also exerts less pressure on the animals.

2. **Step on bare rock** rather than on a living organism wherever possible.

3. **Explore along the exposed beach** or from the edge of a tidepool rather than venturing intothe water. This will provide better viewing conditions and allow animals to remain undisturbed.

4. **Turn over only small rocks** and do so gently. A quick turnover may crush animals that are next to the rock or darting under the rock as their hiding place is uncovered.

5. **Wet your hands with seawater** from the beach before touching or holding an animal exposed by the tide.

How many of these things can you spot on the beach? What other things can you find?

- ☐ Agates
- ☐ Barnacles
- ☐ Crab/coal
- ☐ Driftwood
- ☐ Eagle feather
- ☐ Fossils
- ☐ Glass
- ☐ Heart rocks
- ☐ Ice
- ☐ Jellyfish
- ☐ Kelp
- ☐ Limpets
- ☐ Mussels

- ☐ Net
- ☐ Oyster shells
- ☐ Pacific Ocean
- ☐ Quartz
- ☐ Rocks
- ☐ Seastar
- ☐ Tide pool
- ☐ Urchin
- ☐ Volcanic rocks
- ☐ Whelks
- ☐ Xtratuf Boots
- ☐ Yuck (Thanks for helping clean up the beach!)

- ☐ Zigzags
- ☐ _____
- ☐ _____
- ☐ _____
- ☐ _____
- ☐ _____
- ☐ _____
- ☐ _____
- ☐ _____
- ☐ _____
- ☐ _____
- ☐ _____
- ☐ _____

Made in the USA
Columbia, SC
01 September 2022